FAMILY

WEDDING
ETIQUETTE

FAMILY MATTERS

✓

WEDDING ETIQUETTE

ANGELA LANSBURY

WARD LOCK

First published in 1990 by Ward Lock,
Villiers House, 41–47 Strand, London WC2N 5JE
125 East 23rd Street, Suite 300, New York 10010, USA
A Cassell imprint

Reprinted 1990

Text filmset by Columns of Reading
Printed and bound in Scotland by
William Collins Sons & Co Ltd, Glasgow

British Library Cataloguing in Publication Data
Lansbury, Angela
    Wedding etiquette. — (Family matters)
    1. Wedding planning
    I. Title   II. Series
    395′.22

    ISBN 0–7063–6868–1

CONTENTS

INTRODUCTION

This book gives you the correct form and behaviour for many types of wedding – helping you to organize or attend civil weddings in register offices, church weddings of different Christian denominations, plus Jewish, Sikh and other religious ceremonies without fear of embarassment.

When you are in doubt about what to wear and say, or where and when to stand and sit, guidelines are useful. On the 'big day', when nerves are often strained after weeks of preparation, minor details of procedure can seem immensely important. While planning my own wedding I was surprised at the number of traditional rules that came to light, such as 'First cousins must be invited to the wedding breakfast, but not second cousins', let alone the seeming jungle of priorities and 'pecking orders' involved in seating plans for the ceremony and reception.

IS ETIQUETTE STILL NECESSARY?

When you know the rules they seem logical and you may imagine that nobody needs to be told. But not everyone is supremely confident on matters of etiquette: when I spoke on radio phone-ins, brides and best men reported many etiquette disputes and disasters narrowly averted. So a knowledge of traditional rules and modern variations, plus some advice from professionals, can save you worry, and ensure success.

Nowadays, etiquette is flexible and after checking what usually happens, you can adapt the norm to suit your particular circumstances or can opt to do things differently and even start a new fashion. Just remember the most important old rules of etiquette, that all should be considered and thanked and no-one should be offended.

THE ENGAGEMENT

In Victorian days a man courting an unmarried girl would have approached the family for permission to marry her and would have only proposed once the consent had been given. Today most couples are living fairly independent lives by the time they agree to marry and family pressure is unlikely to be able to separate them. However, legally, you have to be sixteen before you can marry and in England you need parental consent (or a guardian's consent) when marrying a girl or boy under the age of eighteen. If parental consent is unreasonably withheld, you can apply for a court order.

ENGAGEMENT RINGS

A couple may discuss the possibility of getting married, but when an engagement ring of value has been handed over, the young man has made a commitment, and the bride-to-be and onlookers can see that there is an official engagement. The engagement ring is worn on the third finger of the fiancée's left hand because the Greeks thought this finger was connected to the heart. The Romans introduced engagement rings and after they converted to Christianity a 9th-century Pope stipulated that engagement rings must be worn.

An engagement ring may also demonstrate financial

security. Some religious groups (e.g. Jews) require engagement or wedding rings of value to show the husband's ability to support a family. Others accept a ring of no value or no ring at all (e.g. Quakers).

In olden times the groom was supposed to propose in a romantic location on bended knee, presenting his bride-to-be with a ring. The current custom is for the husband-to-be to propose first and then take the bride-to-be to choose her own ring at a jeweller's shop once he has been accepted.

☆ The groom could visit the jeweller in advance and establish the acceptable price range to avoid later embarrassment. If the groom has not done this the bride should avoid opting for an outrageously expensive ring unless she is quite sure that her fiancé can afford it.

ANNOUNCING THE ENGAGEMENT

Once you are engaged, you want to share the good news with everyone you know.

TELLING THE FAMILY

Nowadays, whether the groom asks the bride's father for permission or merely informs him of the engagement depends on various factors, including the bride's age. A young man without his own home and a reasonable income would do well to discuss the matter with his own parents. Their advice or offers of finance may help him approach her parents successfully.

An older man would probably get the girl's agreement first. Then she tells her parents the good news. Having established that his offer is accepted, he can confidently inform his parents.

Both families may want to meet quickly. His family could invite hers home for a general celebration and her family may reciprocate to start discussing wedding arrangements. Or her family can take the initiative.

After the family, close friends are informed by phone or letter before the general newspaper announcement.

TELLING AN EX-GIRLFRIEND OR BOYFRIEND

Very personal communications such as this are supposed to be delivered in person, if you can trust yourself and your former loved one to remain polite and dignified. When phoning to explain avoid opening by saying, 'I've decided to get married.' A girlfriend who doesn't know there is someone else in your life might think you are proposing to her!

If you write, avoid sending a negative letter explaining in detail why you do not want to marry the person you are writing to. Your letter should convey warm, positive feelings about your past relationship and express the view that you wish to remain friends.

You may all meet later in life, so try to remain cordial for everyone's sake. When you write you could include an invitation to the engagement party. The ex might bring along a new love, or find romance amongst your single friends. Sample letter:

Dear Bob,

You have been such a close friend of mine that you are the first person I must tell that Romeo Montagu and I have decided to get engaged. I know that you care for me very much, as I do for you, so I do hope that you will be pleased for me…

NEWSPAPER ANNOUNCEMENTS

The bride's family usually pays for the announcements in their area and in national secular or religious newspapers, but the families of the bride and groom could split the bill, the groom's family placing announcements in their local papers. Formal newspaper announcements in national newspapers such as *The Times*, *The Daily Telegraph* or *The Independent* follow a similar set style which can be brief. *The Times* is read all over the world and carries announcements for weddings in the UK and abroad of all religions. The following will appear in the section called 'Forthcoming Marriage Announcements':

> **Mr A. B. Smith**
> **and Mrs Y. Brown**
> The marriage will take place shortly between Mr Alfred Ben Smith of Harrow, Middlesex, and Mrs Yolanda Brown of Reading, Berkshire.

> **Mr B. C. Smith**
> **and Miss B. A. Brown**
> The engagement is announced between Brian Christopher, son of Mr and Mrs John Smith, of Wiltshire, and Brenda Anne, daughter of Mr A. Brown, MSc, and Mrs Brown, of Bristol.
> The wedding will take place in February in Bristol.

> **Mr A. B. Smith**
> **and Miss Y. Z. Brown**
> The engagement is announced
> between Albert, younger son of
> the late Sir Albert Smith, and of
> the Lady Grey, Lancashire, and
> Yolanda, youngest daughter of
> Dr Jim Brown, of Australia, and
> Mrs Anne Wise of Virginia,
> United States.

You can phone *The Times'* Court and Social advertising department for details of prices and advice on wording. But they must receive notification in writing with the signature of bride or groom or one of the parents and the address to which the bill will be sent.

'Son of' or 'daughter of' usually means the only son or the only daughter, though you can state 'only son of'. 'Younger' means younger of two. 'Youngest' means youngest of three or more, while 'elder' means elder of two, 'eldest' of three or more. 'Third son/daughter' can be inserted if there are several.

ENGAGEMENT OF STEPCHILDREN

If the groom's father is dead and his mother remarried, state 'Peter, son of the late Mr John Brown, stepson of Mr Graham Jones'. If Peter's mother was still married to Mr John Brown at the time of John's death you say, 'son of the late Mr John Brown and Mrs Brown'. If she was already divorced from John when he died say 'Peter, son of the late Mr John Brown and Mrs Anne Brown'. If Anne had remarried Graham Jones before John Brown died you say 'Peter, son of the late Mr John Brown and Mrs Graham Jones'.

LETTER OF CONGRATULATION

After reading newspaper announcements.

> 12 Artillery Avenue,
> Edinburgh,
> Scotland.
>
> Dear Juliet,
> I opened the Times newspaper today and was
> delighted to hear that you are getting married.
> We seem to have lost touch in the past few
> months while I have been abroad/taking exams/
> living up north/but I have often thought about you.
> If you can spare a moment I would love to know
> how you met Romeo, and about your plans.
> Wishing you a long and happy married life,
>
> Anne

The bride-to-be can reply by phone and send an invitation to the engagement party or wedding.

THE ENGAGEMENT PARTY

The engagement party takes place when the ring has been bought, as soon as possible so everyone can meet the proposed other half.

ENGAGEMENT PARTY INVITATIONS

For a large formal seated dinner printed cards look better and save time. Stationery shops and printers have examples of typefaces. For formal occasions wording is in the third person as if a secretary is writing on behalf of the hostess. For an informal party you can buy pre-printed invitation cards and fill in the blanks. Invitations read:

Mr & Mrs Mark Capulet
request the pleasure of the company of

....

at an engagement party
to celebrate the engagement of
Juliet Capulet and Romeo Montagu
on Saturday January 1st at 8pm at
The Cottage, Little Village, Surrey.

Mrs M Capulet
1 Mansion House
High Street
London SW1
Tel: 01-123 4567   *RSVP*

Newsagents and stationers stock pads of colourful illustrated engagement party invitations suitable for a young person's party or a buffet.

These invitations are usually in the first person. A typical form of wording is:

> *To* ....
> *Please join us to celebrate our engagement*
> *Time* ....
> *Place* ....
> *From* ....
> *RSVP*

You fill in the blanks.

A hand-written note from the couple can be in the first or third person and begins:

> *Juliet Capulet and Romeo Montagu*
> *invite you/John Brown to a party*
> *to celebrate their engagement*
> *on July.........*

Include the home address for the RSVP if it is different from the party location.

REPLY TO AN ENGAGEMENT PARTY INVITATION

If no reply card is included, reply in the first or third person following the style of the invitation. In the first person you begin 'Thank you very much for your ...' If the invitation is in the third person, you should reply in the third person:

> *John Brown thanks Mr and Mrs Capulet for their kind invitation to the engagement party of Juliet Capulet and Romeo Montagu to be held on Saturday January 1st at 8pm at The Cottage, Little Village, Surrey, which he has much pleasure in accepting.*

To decline, you say, for example, 'which he regrets he is unable to accept owing to absence abroad'.

State the time, place and date. The hosts are unlikely to be holding two engagement parties, but they might hold two parties in the same month, and if they wrote the wrong date on your invitation or you misread their writing they will be able to warn you.

PARTY VENUE

The engagement party can be held at the girl's parents' home, or a hall, and there may be another party for the young people at her flat.

Guests take gifts which will be useful in a new home. No speeches are necessary though at large gatherings with seated dinners somebody usually stands at the end to toast the VIPs — the happy couple — and thank the hosts. The hosts stand near the door at the end of the party to say goodbye and be thanked.

CANCELLING THE ENGAGEMENT

Jitters and doubts can occur and the chief bridesmaid and best man should offer moral support when the volume of organization and family diplomacy required seems overwhelming. Ministers of religion, doctors and other advisers often use phrases such as, 'Don't worry, it's such a huge step, affecting your whole life, that most people occasionally wonder if they're doing the right thing.'

Avoid arguments within your family and between the two sides. Conflicts occur if she insists on living in the centre of town when he can only afford a suburban house, or his parents complain that a buffet will not be enough for their relatives travelling across the country. A Midlands wedding went ahead despite the boy's parents' refusal to attend because they thought that the girl wasn't good enough for him. There is always hope that the couple's parents may be reconciled when their first grandchild is born. However, sometimes an engagement is cancelled.

WORDING OF CANCELLED ENGAGEMENT ANNOUNCEMENT

Newspaper announcements simply state the names and say that the wedding will not take place. Strictly speaking, it should be implied that the girl has broken off the engagement. She might have had second thoughts after being persuaded to accept a flattering proposal immediately. It would reflect badly on him if it seemed that he rashly proposed to every girlfriend then heartlessly changed his mind. It would also be uncivil of him to imply that on knowing the girl better he decided she was unsuitable to be his wife, and by implication anyone else's.

An announcement by letter could go as follows:

Alice and I are very fond of each other but after serious heart-searching she/we decided that our aims in life are so different that it would not be right for us to get married at this time. We are sorry if changing our plans has disappointed those close to us, but feel that by separating for a while/by staying just good friends, in the long run we will both be happier.

RETURN OF RING

The Church originally demanded that a man or woman who broke their promise forfeited the ring. Grandparents may tell you the Victorian ruling that if he cancelled the engagement she was entitled to keep the ring. He was lucky if the girl's father did not sue him for breach of promise and the hurt girl was content with a pretty ring as consolation. It is not done to give somebody a present and ask for it back, but if the boy has cancelled, many girls will not want to keep a ring which reminds them of a broken engagement and often return it anyway.

If she cancels the engagement she returns the ring, which he can – if he so chooses – give to a future fiancée. The general rule nowadays is return the ring because engagements are shorter than they used to be. Obviously if the girl is given a ring and the next morning she changes her mind she must return the ring. However, if she wears the ring for years and has grown used to it the situation is different.

RETURNING WEDDING GIFTS

After an engagment is broken, gifts for a new home are not needed. Gifts sent in advance by wedding guests must be returned, preferably in person. This gives relatives the chance to express dismay or relief and offer consolation along the lines of, 'Never mind. It seems hard now, but you may end up marrying someone even nicer. I hope you do.'

☆ Resist the temptation to say, 'I never liked him/her. I always thought he/she was an ugly, stuck-up, ... !' You never know, they might get back together next week!

☆ If the wedding goes ahead or the young man quickly finds another bride, the stored present might be given to him again. However, the second bride-to-be may have a different wedding list.

WEDDING DECISIONS

SETTING THE WEDDING DATE

Once you are engaged, friends will ask when you are getting married. You might wait until college studies finish, but it is embarrassing when no date is agreed. A young man who cannot set up home should not remain engaged indefinitely but should leave the girl free to meet someone else. Shorter engagements are more common nowadays because couples with incomes and savings can borrow money from mortgage companies. (See the companion volume to this one *The Wedding Planner* for further advice on choosing a date.)

CHOOSING ATTENDANTS

The wedding group consists of the bride and groom and their nearest relatives, parents, and brothers and sisters. The bride is given away in church by her father. When the father is deceased or too ill to attend, she can be given away by a brother, uncle, cousin or friend of the family.

The best man can be the groom's brother, cousin, friend, father, or even his mother. Ushers are not needed in a small register office. The immediate family naturally sit right at the front. Others sit further away, and order does not matter because there is nothing very dramatic to see and those at the back are not at a great distance.

NUMBERS OF ATTENDANTS NEEDED

Are bridesmaids necessary? Not always. It is nice to give your pretty unmarried sister a chance to dress up and share in the wedding day at a church wedding with a procession. The bride wearing a dress with a long white train needs assistance. It would be desirable to have a bridesmaid or two at a big wedding with several ushers. Numbers of bridesmaids need not match the numbers of ushers exactly. He may have two brothers, while she has only one sister. Family are chosen before friends. A chief bridesmaid or matron-of-honour is appointed to take charge of younger bridesmaids.

CHOOSING SPEECHMAKERS

The main speeches are usually given by the father of the bride, the groom and best man. But other members of the family, friends or important guests who make good speeches can be substituted. (See notes on speeches in the section on 'Reception', page 82).

INVITING WEDDING GUESTS

It is natural and courteous for the host to invite an equal proportion of guests from each family. However, if the wedding is at the bride's family home in another town, the groom's family may require fewer invitations. The host, traditionally the bride's father, decides how much he is prepared to pay and how many can be seated at both the ceremony and at the hall he has chosen. It is quite usual when space is at a premium at the ceremony to invite guests to the reception only.

To accommodate a larger number of guests from either side a separate informal and less expensive party can be held at home. (Sometimes the engagement party is a means of inviting all those friends and colleagues who you cannot invite to the wedding for reasons of both space and expense). The minimum for a small wedding is the two witnesses, plus parents and brothers and sisters of bride and groom if they live nearby, are on good terms and approve of the wedding. Larger weddings involve cousins, children, friends, family, colleagues and acquaintances.

WORDING OF WEDDING INVITATIONS

A good printer will supply an appropriate typeface and embossed print or hand-engraved print, and appropriate reply cards if required. Printers offer a choice of styles at various prices.

Old rules say that for major events such as births, engagements, marriages and deaths you should reply in writing because printing is too impersonal. However, most people don't have the time or the staff to send out 150 handwritten invitations, or write numerous handwritten letters.

The invitation is from the hosts:

Mr & Mrs Arthur Bridesparents
request the honour
of your company
at the marriage of their daughter
Jaqueline Yvonne
to
Mr Robert Adam Groom
at St Mary's Church, Twickenham, Middlesex
on Saturday 27 October at 11.30am
and afterwards at The Garden Hotel,
Twickenham, Middlesex.

7 Crown Avenue
Twickenham
Middlesex   RSVP

RECEPTION ONLY INVITATION

A separate printed invitation is issued to the wedding reception. This enables many people to be invited to a large church but only a few to a small hall where there is a seated meal. Or you might invite few to a small register office and many to a large buffet afterwards:

---

*Please join us at a reception/disco party
to celebrate the marriage of
Juliet Capulet and Romeo Montagu
at 6pm on Saturday July 1st
at The Cottage, Little Village, Surrey.
Dinner 7pm
Dress Informal*

*Mrs D Capulet
1 Mansion House
High Street
London SW1
Tel: 01-123 4567*   *RSVP*

It is a good idea to make it clear to guests what sort of reception you are giving. People who were expecting a quick drink down at the pub and a few sandwiches after the ceremony might be somewhat taken aback to find themselves invited to an elaborate sit-down silver service meal. They may not have worn the right clothes or made adequate arrangements for taking time off work or getting a babysitter for several hours.

Your invitation could be worded:

... reception/drinks at 6 pm, dinner at 8 pm at Trumps Manor House Hotel, RSVP.'

or

... to a buffet lunch afterwards at Sherry Cottage, RSVP.'

☆ The meal after a wedding is traditionally known as the 'wedding breakfast'. This does not mean that it is a breakfast consisting of bacon and eggs. It can be a lunch, buffet or dinner, but it is called a breakfast because the bride and groom are breaking their fast – having their first meal together as a married couple, with their guests.

WEDDING STATIONERY

For less formal weddings you can buy pads of invitations. The usual wording is:

'... (name) and ... (name) request the pleasure of your company ...' or 'the pleasure of your company is requested at the marriage of ... (name) to celebrate the marriage of ... (name) at ... (time and place)'.

Order extra invitations to allow for those wrongly addressed or gone astray. When guests decline because of sickness or holidays, extra invitations must be sent quickly, so additional guests won't feel second best.

INDICATING CORRECT DRESS FOR GUESTS

For a daytime wedding, formal clothes will be morning suit (black or grey) for the men, and elegant knee-length day dresses for the women. At all but the most formal weddings it is now acceptable for men to wear a smart suit instead.

Nowadays many couples do not leave for their honeymoon immediately but spend the night nearby, and hold an evening dinner. For an evening dinner, evening dress may be worn. 'Black tie' means black tie and black dinner jacket for men and evening dresses for ladies. 'Dress optional' means you don't mind whether guests wear evening dress or not. If they have evening dress or like dressing up they can wear evening dress, but guests need not feel obliged to spend time and money buying a special outfit or hiring one, nor stay away because they don't have the right clothes. Give a phone number to allow anyone in doubt to phone and ascertain the time, type of dinner, and correct dress.

INVITING CHILDREN

When inviting guests to bring their children do not write 'and family', which sounds as if you cannot remember their children. Name each child invited. If you cannot remember, phone ostensibly to check the family's postcode, asking polite questions about the children's school progress. Note the names.

Bridesmaids and pageboys do not have to be relatives. They can be any children the bride and groom are fond of, or who care a lot about them. An Australian nanny had her small boy and girl charges acting as bridesmaid and ringbearer.

Large numbers of children, such as a teacher's primary school class or a ballet class, can be given a special role as the guard of honour. They could carry arches of ribbons and flowers for the bride and groom to walk through.

Some people prefer not to have children (particularly those under five) at their wedding. Although this is perfectly understandable, it would cause less offence to ring the parents personally and explain the situation rather than putting only the parents' names on the invitation and a cryptic note such as 'sorry, no children invited'. If there are several couples with children whom you would really like at the wedding and who cannot arrange babysitting, it may be that after talking to them you could organize some crèche facilities at the reception venue.

REPLIES TO INVITATIONS

Nowadays hosts send printed reply cards and stamped addressed envelopes with invitations so that guests can reply promptly, simply deleting 'accepts with pleasure' or 'is unable to accept'. As with engagement party invitations described above, when you receive a wedding invitation in the third person the correct form for replying is in the third person. John Brown has much pleasure in accepting ... etc.

THE STAG PARTY

The timing of the stag party is crucial. It should *not* be held the night before the wedding ceremony. One groom got drunk, walked into a lamp-post, and had a black eye at the wedding and on the photographs. A late night out drinking before such a major event is inconsiderate to the worried bride, and a hangover makes it harder for the best man to do his best on the wedding day. The best man has a duty to ensure that the groom arrives at the church on time, and is sober at the wedding reception.

The best man usually organizes the stag party, unless he lives in another town. If you are having a drink at the local pub the groom does not pay. Guests can pay for their own drinks. The best man might buy the first round.

As a guest, you might like to mark the occasion by presenting a small gift or card,

'To John,
Congratulations on your engagement.
Wishing you every happiness.
From your friends Mark, Tom, Sam and Anthony.'

Organize a handclap or sing, 'For He's A Jolly Good

Fellow.' Raise your glasses and drink a toast, 'To Peter,' or 'To Peter and Janie!'.

STAG PARTY ENTERTAINMENT

If you have non-drinking friends you are in luck. You have some drivers. The best man should buy the drivers non-alcoholic drinks such as fruit juice and coffee or alcohol-free lager. The best man might offer to pay for the petrol, or split the cost of the petrol and buy the drivers' food. If the drivers won't accept, the best man can order sandwiches or food for everyone including the drivers.

FORMAL SPEECHES FOR STAG PARTIES

For a good evening out the best man might plan a sit-down dinner at a restaurant. Alternatively have wives and girlfriends gathering in another room or a wine bar for a hen party, and all meet later. He could make a brief, humorous toast, preferably involving the personalities of the bride and groom and wish the groom and his bride a happy future.

At a formal stag party the first main speech is made by the best man. The reply is made by the groom. More details and suggestions are given in *How To Be The Best Man*, also in this series.

WHO DOES WHAT

★ *THE BRIDE*   The bride chooses her bridesmaids, her own dress, the colours of the bridesmaids' dresses, and the flower colours. All her work is done in advance. On the day she is 'Queen for the day' and is not obliged to do much except look decorative, repeat the vows, sign her name, throw her bouquet and chat to her guests. The chief bridesmaid may help her to dress, the chauffeur opens the car door, her father leads her up the aisle, and her husband makes the speech.

★ **THE BRIDE'S MOTHER**

She organizes the catering for a young bride and advises on everything else too. She dresses elegantly, and is given a corsage to distinguish her.

★ **THE BRIDE'S FATHER**

He escorts the bride in the procession and the bride's mother-in-law in the recession. He pays for the reception, and often makes a speech, usually the first speech. He is in clothing co-ordinated with the groom. He may be doing behind-the-scenes managing such as paying caterers. Being host and most senior he invisibly settles queries immediately or postpones disputes with staff until later. Therefore neither bride nor groom, nor bride's mother should have their day spoilt by uncertainty, and the guests, too, are undisturbed.

★ **THE GROOM'S MOTHER**

The groom's mother advises if asked, dresses in smart fashion similar to the bride's mother, taking care to choose a different colour, wears a corsage for identification, and is an honoured guest.

★ **THE GROOM'S
FATHER**

He wears similar attire to the groom and groom's family, because he, too, is an honoured guest.

★ **THE BEST MAN**

He may help the groom dress. He is responsible for arranging transport of the groom to the church, carrying the ring, paying church fees, possibly signing as witness, escorting the chief bridesmaid in the recession, arranging transport for everyone from the church to the reception, making a speech, and handing over honeymoon documents.

★ **THE USHERS**

They seat guests at church, help the best man with transport and are generally helpful to the groom and best man. Ushers show guests to seats in church, hand out order-of-service sheets and organize transport and parking. They wear formal wedding party clothes and buttonhole flowers for identification.

★ **THE CHIEF
BRIDESMAID**

She may help the bride to dress and soothe her nerves on the morning of the wedding. At the wedding she holds the bride's bouquet, and organizes younger bridesmaids and pageboys. She may also assist the bride by holding the bride's gloves, prayerbook, handbag, signing the register as witness, and partnering the best man in the recession. Younger bridesmaids assist the bride, sometimes carrying her train. The chief bridesmaid may take charge of wedding clothes when the bride changes.

★ *THE TOAST-MASTER*

He announces the names of guests approaching the receiving line, asks for silence for the minister to say grace before meals, introduces speechmakers who will make toasts, reads telegrams, calls for the cake-cutting, and the first dance.

PLANNING THE RECEPTION

Wherever you decide to hold your wedding reception – in a hotel or in a hired marquee – ensure that you know exactly what you expect people to do.

TOP TABLE SEATING FOR A FORMAL MEAL

The main rule is that the bride and groom are seated in the middle of the table so that everyone can see them. Their parents are next, finally the attendants – the best man and chief bridesmaid at the end.

The order is man, woman, man, woman, alternating. Like the bride and groom, male and female members of the two sides of the family are paired, as in the recession.

STANDARD SEATING

The bride has her husband on her right, her father on her left. The groom has his mother-in-law on his right. She has the groom's father on her right. The groom's mother is at the other end next to the bride's father. But the groom's mother is not on the end of the table because the best man is next to her. Usually the table seats no more than eight or ten. If there is no bridesmaid the bride is in the centre. If there is a bridesmaid, the bridesmaid sits at the end next to the groom's father.

You may have room for grandparents, then another bridesmaid and usher or the minister with his wife at the end. But the best man's wife or girlfriend and the bridesmaid's boyfriend do not belong on the top table, nor do stepfathers and spouses who took no part in the wedding ceremony. You could place all the attendants on a separate young guests' table. For a double wedding you merely place the two brides and grooms in the centre.

MODERN WEDDING RECEPTIONS

An older couple may pay for and organize their own reception. This is because their parents may be too old to do so or are no longer alive. The older couple are probably earning money or have savings. They will want to make their own decisions.

PARENTS' SECOND MARRIAGES

The role of the bride's stepfather varies according to circumstances. If the bride's father died long ago and the stepfather is affectionately regarded like a real father, then he takes the same role that a real father would, pays for the wedding, and stands in the receiving line at the hall with the bride's mother. The only difference will be the names on the invitation, making it clear that he is the bride's stepfather and she is the daughter of the late Mr So and So. This is essential, both out of courtesy to the bride's father's relatives and so that the groom's relatives or guests do not get confused and inadvertently say the bride looks just like her stepfather or stepbrothers.

If the bride's own father is alive and he, too, has remarried, his second wife is merely a guest. She has not helped the bride organize the wedding preparations. She does not want to be in the receiving line being congratulated on a daughter who is not hers or a wedding she has not organized. She should probably dress fairly inconspicuously, say little to avoid being misconstrued, keep at a discreet distance, and leave before numbers dwindle. Alternatively, depending on how amicable relationships are, she can feign illness or business or travel abroad and not attend but send polite thanks for the invitation and good wishes to the bride and groom.

When the bride's natural father is paying for the wedding, his name goes on the invitations, and he is the host in the receiving line welcoming guests, one of whom is the stepfather. The wedding invitation can mention the names of both father and stepfather, making it clear to which the bride's mother is currently married, who is the father of the bride, and who is the host.

If the bride's mother has suffered an acrimonious divorce, should the bride's real father be invited? In most cases, it would probably serve no purpose and could even ruin the day if someone caused a scene after too much champagne. Since it is the bride's day, it should be left up to her to invite her father and encourage him to bury the hatchet for one afternoon for her sake. In any case, a parent's ex-spouse should be informed of the wedding but it should be made very clear if their attendance is unwanted. The same is true of the ex-spouse of a bride or groom who is remarrying.

BRIDE'S OR GROOM'S SECOND MARRIAGE

An ex-wife or ex-husband who has remarried may be relieved that you are remarrying, providing the children's welfare is assured. The Decree Nisi is not made absolute until the judge is satisfied that children of the former marriage are provided for. It is tempting to tell other relatives, hoping they'll spread your news. However, don't let young children make revelations and risk suffering angry reactions.

When a second marriage is planned, the children must be told by their parents. It is a nice gesture to make small stepchildren feel part of the wedding ceremony, providing this does not make their natural, divorced parent feel betrayed, forcing children to take sides. Sensitive teenagers who feel neglected can be given prominence as bridesmaids, best man, or usher.

The ex-spouse's parents must be informed about the wedding. Many people remain on very good terms with an ex-spouse's parents. In this case it would be correct to invite them to the wedding. But they may feel awkward and undecided about whether they ought to attend. Perhaps you could pen a brief note such as, 'I/We will understand if you feel you should not attend. However, if you would like to be present we shall be very happy to see you.'

The ex in-laws might attend but depart early, perhaps taking the children back to their home to spend the night. Work out how you are going to introduce the in-laws and where they will sit if there is a seated meal. The problem is solved if the children say, 'this is my other granny, Granny Jenny', or if you seat them next to people they already know well, such as ex next-door neighbours.

BRIDE'S SECOND MARRIAGE

For a bride's second marriage it is not usual for her to

wear white, or a veil, or have bridesmaids. She can, however, have a matron-of-honour. Care must be taken to consider the stepchildren's roles. Speeches must be tactful. (See *Wedding Speeches & Toasts*, also in this series).

The receiving line will be different and smaller than for a first wedding. At a small wedding, when the bride and groom are hosts in their new home, they stand by the door to welcome guests. The best man and matron-of-honour hover behind directing guests to the drinks.

At the wedding breakfast the friends from the time of the former marriage are best kept together.

POSTPONED AND MODIFIED WEDDINGS

Reasons for postponing a wedding include illness or death in the family. An announcement must be sent out. The newspaper announcement reads: Mrs X regrets that owing to the illness of Mr X/death of the late Mr Y the wedding of Ann X to Bill Y on (date) has been postponed/will take place quietly.

Revised wedding plans might include modified music and dancing, and less elaborate clothes. Honeymoon plans can be changed if a quieter honeymoon is preferred to jollity, or so that a widowed or worried mother is not alone for long.

CORRECT DRESS

What you wear at a wedding is one of the most important decisions of the day, whether you are the bride, a member of the wedding party, or a guest.

THE BRIDE'S DRESS

The popular style is ankle length. When the wedding takes place in a church (or synagogue) the dress often follows old-fashioned convention, covering the bride up to the neck and down to the ankles and wrists, though the dress may have see-through net areas from bust to collar.

Summer dresses may have shorter sleeves and lower necklines. Colours can be white or off-white or pastel colours such as creamy yellow, baby pink, pale blue, or lavender. The bride can wear ribbons in her hair and on her dress echoing the colours of the bridesmaids' dresses.

Some churches object to brides wearing bright red, which is unconventional and can look garish. In olden days red had associations with the devil and prostitution. Few people nowadays remember or care about such symbolism because fashionable colours change every season.

The tradition of wearing a white dress is, contrary to popular belief, a relatively recent one. Before the invention of the sewing machine in the mid-nineteenth century, all clothes were considered too expensive to be worn only once, so brides tended to marry in everyday best clothes. Although white is now the favourite colour for first-timers, second-time brides or those closer to forty than twenty, tend to marry in a more expensive version of a day-dress in a pastel colour.

DRESS MATERIAL

Lace is favoured because it is pretty, delicate, decorative, and expensive. Nottingham lace is obviously what you should wear if you live in that area and have close relatives working in the industry.

Evening dress material is shiny and elaborate so that it can be seen under dim lighting. Ordinary cotton is lightweight and cool for a summer afternoon dress, but a more glamorous material is better for grand weddings. Bridal dress shops sell white satin flat or heeled shoes.

☆ The bride's dress is kept a secret for good luck, and is not seen before the wedding. This ensures that everyone has a lovely surprise. For the same reason the bride is not seen by the groom on the day of the wedding until she appears at church.

THE BRIDE'S VEIL

The veil dates back to biblical times in the Middle East. The bride wore a veil for modesty. She walks up the aisle with her face modestly concealed. When the veil is removed by her groom, herself, or her bridesmaid, at the altar before signing the register, the groom is the first to see her. She returns down the aisle with the veil thrown back and all the guests can see her smiling. The veil is usually attached to a circlet made of similar material to the dress, with pearls, flowers, lace or other decoration. A bride can also wear her hair up, secured with a lattice of white ribbons or flowers. This looks particularly effective against dark hair.

BRIDE'S MAKE-UP

Professional make-up artists can be employed for a wedding. They often go for a more subtle effect than the bride might like. The bride may feel tempted to exaggerate her eyes with centipede false black eyelashes, or wear heavy red lipstick or lashings of crimson blusher. Professional make-up may be disappointing at the time, but it produces a more elegant, natural effect in photographs, and looks less dated in years to come.

BRIDE'S ACCESSORIES

The belt of a day dress can match the dress material or the accessories. A neater appearance is gained by matching accessories. Shoes and handbag can be dyed the same colour.

If the dress has small false pearls sewn on it, ear-rings or pearl droplets can be worn to match, and pearls on the shoes. Pearls are said to resemble tears and therefore to be unlucky. But if you are not superstitious and you like pearls, by all means wear them. Jewellery and watches should be in similar styles and of like metals – such as all gold or all silver. Don't wear a watch with a plastic or mangled brown leather strap and a scratched watchface. Even if you are on a low budget you can find smart, reasonably priced evening-style watches with white, black or metal straps, and imitation diamonds around the watchface. Sometimes father or mother can lend a spare analogue watch which looks suitable with period clothes.

☆ Wear: 'Something Old, Something New, Something Borrowed, Something Blue, and a Sixpence in your Shoe'. The borrowed item represents friendship, and the blue is for faithfulness. The sixpence (or fivepence) in the shoe symbolizes never being without money.

BRIDE'S JEWELLERY

The minimum of jewellery is worn, perhaps because the puritanical tradition of the Reformation says you do not glitter too much in an Anglican church. Besides, you do not want to distract attention from the ring.

The engagement ring is worn on the left hand to go with the wedding ring. You can simply leave it off for the day if you like.

☆ A divorcee removes her previous wedding ring. She might wear the old wedding ring before acquiring the new one because she is used to wearing a ring or doesn't want people to think she is an unmarried mother. But it looks odd to wear two wedding rings and may remind her new husband on the day that he is number two. A wedding ring can be remodelled with a stone to make a dress ring.

BRIDE'S INFORMAL CLOTHES

Marrying in a register office allows greater freedom of dress than a church wedding where revealing low necks or very bright colours would seem irreverent at a place of worship.

A bride at a register office wedding usually wears a smart day-dress, or a suit with a hat, or even a trouser suit, but there is no reason why she cannot wear the traditional long white dress if she wants to.

☆ Some register offices have a room where the bride can change her outfit. A bride who marries in a long white dress with a heavy train will need a going-away outfit if she is departing to the airport or on public transport the same day.

WIDOW'S WEDDING CLOTHES

Widows may well be merry about getting married again, but they are not supposed to look gleefully triumphant, as if the first husband has at last passed away and the real fun has begun. So a matron-of-honour is acceptable, but no crowds of angelic bridesmaids. The bride might have a neat corsage, rather than a showy bouquet.

CORRECT DRESS FOR THE GROOM AND ATTENDANTS

All attendants should be clear and liaise about what to wear: it's easy if you know the rules.

★ *THE GROOM*   In theory, for a formal wedding the groom should wear morning dress. This means a grey or black swallowtail coat, striped trousers and a grey silk hat. If he does wear this outfit the rest of the groom's party, including the best man, bride's father, groom's father and ushers, should also be in morning dress. In reality this can be a very costly business since most men do not have a morning suit in their wardrobe and so have to hire one. Although morning dress does make the occasion extra special, many people opt instead for a smart dark suit which they will be able to wear again.

★ **THE BEST MAN**

The best man's accessories – such as his carnation – should distinguish him from the groom (he doesn't want the bride's distant cousins congratulating him) and from the ushers.

★ **THE USHERS**

If you decide to hire morning suits you might prefer that all the ushers look identical. Grey is a safe colour. To create a co-ordinated look the groom might buy the ushers matching ties and handkerchiefs. Their buttonhole flowers should all be the same colour.

★ **THE BRIDES-MAIDS**

The chief bridesmaid, especially if she is of similar age to the bride, must be dressed so that strangers can tell which is the bride. She can wear a more sophisticated style than younger bridesmaids, but in the same or similar colour. The matron-of-honour's clothes are more suited to an older married woman, e.g. a smart suit and hat, with a corsage co-ordinating with the bride's bouquet colour perhaps, showing her role as a member of the wedding party.

Bridesmaids should all wear the same colour material for a co-ordinated look, with matching or contrasting shoes. Accessories can be in a colour that matches the ushers' buttonhole flowers, ties, pocket handkerchiefs, or that cummerbunds can echo.

GUESTS' CLOTHES FOR A FORMAL WEDDING

The time and location of the wedding as well as the size decides how formally you should dress. Religious weddings are more formal than those in a register office.

The invitation wording generally gives an indication of correct dress. A reception after six can mean evening dress. 'Black tie', written on the invitation means men wear a bow tie and black dinner jacket. When men wear black tie the women wear long dresses or evening dresses of current fashion. Guests who find themselves under-dressed can pop home to change if they live nearby. However, the bride may wish to put guests at their ease by saying that clothes are not important. 'I invited you, (guest's name), not your suit!'.

FLOWERS

FLOWERS FOR THE WOMEN

The bride's bouquet is paid for by the groom's family. It can co-ordinate with flowers decorating the church. Two families with weddings at the same place can arrange to share the cost of flowers. The bride may choose the same flowers to decorate the wedding tables. Corsages for the mother and mother-in-law are bought by the groom, and may echo the bride's bouquet, and of course must not clash with the colour of the dresses.

FLOWERS FOR THE MEN

The buttonhole decorations for the ushers are bought by the groom. Usually carnations are worn. The groom might wear a white carnation to echo the bride's dress. Other members of the wedding party might all wear another colour echoing the bridesmaids' dresses, e.g. pink, yellow, cream, or red. One system is for the bride's family to wear white carnations, while the groom's wears red. The men's buttonhole flowers are worn on the left. You cannot go wrong. The man's jacket will have the buttonhole slit on the left.

FLOWER SYMBOLISM

Daffodils mean welcome, orange blossoms signify happiness in marriage, red roses represent love, white roses mean worthy of love, and white carnations are for purity.

TRANSPORT

All cars should arrive five minutes early to ensure punctuality. The outside and inside of the car should be clean, including the boot. Floormats should be clean, ashtrays empty, and the car interior free from smoke. The driver should not smell of smoke, sweat, or alcohol.

★ *MEETING AND GREETING GUESTS* In country areas the bride's family should send cars to meet guests arriving by train. The car driver should go to the platform to help guests with luggage. The driver should explain who he is to avoid confusion. You don't want the groom's friends saying, 'Thank you, my good man,' and giving the bride's grandfather a tip.

★ *THE CHAUFFEUR* The chauffeur of a grand car such as a Rolls-Royce will wear a black tie and shoes and driving gloves. He touches his cap when the passengers arrive. For royalty he removes his hat in their presence except when driving.

The chauffeur is supposed to seat the passengers before stowing luggage, therefore the passengers may get into the car looking nonchalant. But anxious passengers who want to see their luggage stowed before getting into the car should be allowed to check on this. The passenger is king, even if he isn't a king.

★ *THE BRIDAL CAR* In large cities like London some people hire a white Rolls-Royce for the bridal couple, or even have a fleet of Rolls-Royces, stretch limousines, or Mercedes. White is the conventional colour. In London, a white taxi can be hired. But a blue, yellow or even a pink Rolls-Royce or other car is amusing.

Suitably stylish transport should also be provided for the bridal party who travel in convoy after the bridal car. It would look absurd to have the bridal couple in a Rolls with rusting old wrecks following.

Sometimes bridal cars drive along, hooting and blowing vulgar musical tooters to attract attention from passers-by. This sounds fun but it is illegal to hoot except in emergencies.

★ **THE DEPARTURE CAR** If you must have noise, tin cans such as Coke cans can be tied on the back bumper of the car. The elegant clip-clop of horses makes an unusual, arresting sound. A horse-drawn carriage can be hired, which is lovely in fine weather. To look suitably stylish and 'olde worlde' in a carriage the groom can wear a morning coat and a top hat.

Signs written on the car might include Just Married, or the first names of the couple, John and Sue, at the top of the front windows.

WEDDING RULES

You need to know the rules for any wedding in which you are participating. There are different rules for register offices and church weddings in England and Scotland, Wales and Ireland. Within each religion orthodox rules are likely to be stricter than those in less rigid sects.

If guests of other religions attend your wedding, tell them what to expect. Arrange for somebody to greet them and stay with them so they don't feel isolated and awkward. Ensure they can find acceptable food and drink at the reception.

When you are a guest at a wedding of another religion it is a courtesy to know about their religious customs.

CIVIL MARRIAGES

At the moment, a civil marriage must take place in a register office in the area where the bride or groom lives. Directory enquiries will give you details of the nearest. A current Green Paper has new propositions such as couples being able to marry in another area, or in a prettier building designated for marriages by the local authority such as a manor house at extra cost. If you are not getting married for some time, check whether changes have been made.

The register office will be decorated with flowers so you need not provide any. Bride and groom sit or stand by the registrar at the front and there is no particular ruling about seating other guests. Obviously the immediate family want to be nearest. A ring is not strictly necessary, nor are bridesmaids or a best man, just two witnesses, who may be of either sex.

Technically you can get married between 8 am and 6 pm, but register office hours vary between local authorities, and each register office has its own hours. They may be open on Saturday mornings.

Check the amount of advance notice required, and the documents you must provide. These may include the Marriage Notice form, Birth Certificate, Decree of Divorce/Annulment, Death Certificate of former spouse, Certificate of No Impediment for Foreign Residents, and translations of these documents if they are in a foreign language. You need to fill in the forms and supply the documents, and arrange the time for the marriage with the registrar – remembering that his office may be booked up well in advance in spring and summer. You need the two witnesses, and the fee. Fifteen days' minimum notice is required. There is also a three months' maximum.

You must register your intention to marry at a register office over three weeks in advance. This is because while Anglicans (members of the Church of England and allied established churches in Wales) have their intention to get married read in church as official banns (see page 51), those participating in a civil marriage have their intention to get married displayed on a board at the register office.

MARRIAGE ON SHIPS

You cannot be married on the high seas on British ships. Royal Navy personnel can give notice of intention to marry on ships and later marry on shore. You can marry on some foreign ships under foreign marriage laws. If the ship is moored on a river or in a port in Britain this can make a difference. Consult the local registrar's office.

RELIGIOUS CEREMONIES

Many people prefer to be married with a religious ceremony. Although some of the requirements and procedures can seem daunting and overwhelming, once you know the various rules of etiquette it is great fun.

MARRYING A WIDOW/WIDOWER

Traditionally a grieving widow or widower mourns a year before recovering and remarrying. Major stresses in life, a funeral, moving house, and getting married, are a lot to cope with in quick succession, or to inflict on children and relatives not feeling like a jolly wedding. Three months is the minimum decent time. Wedding announcements are made six weeks ahead – barely a month after funeral and memorial services! Besides, you need about six weeks to prepare documentation for the new marriages.

REMARRYING IN CHURCH

A marriage which is declared void or annulled may enable a second wife or husband to marry in church or other religious premises. Marriages can be declared void if one party was under the age of sixteen, had VD, or the woman was pregnant by another man. The objection must be raised within three years by the aggrieved party who was deceived at the time of marriage.

WHO CANNOT MARRY?

CONSANGUINITY

Certain marriages are forbidden as consanguineous or incestuous, because blood relations may increase the risk of medical problems. These are people who are related in a direct line. A man may not marry his mother, daughter, grandmother, grand-daughter, or aunt. Similarly, a woman may not marry her son, father, grandson, grandfather, uncle and so on. You can marry a first cousin or a second cousin, though most people check their family health history first.

AFFINITY

You cannot marry anyone to whom you are closely related through marriage – your ex-wife's or ex-husband's direct relatives. It would create family conflict. A man cannot marry his ex-wife's mother, daughter, and so on. A woman cannot marry her ex-husband's father or son, and so on.

Laws have been relaxed to allow a man to marry the niece of his ex-wife even if the ex-wife is alive. The minister may still refuse to marry you, but might permit you to be married in his church if another clergyman agrees to officiate.

ADOPTION

Marriage to your adopted children is banned. Further details can be found by applying to the registrar's offices. Forbidden marriages are listed in the prayer book.

OUTSIDE CHURCH

Marriages can take place outside a church in special circumstances, e.g. when one of the partners is imprisoned, housebound or confined to hospital. Catholics and Anglicans must marry in a register office or church. If you are a member of another religion you may need a registrar present, or a register office ceremony first. See below.

CHURCH OF ENGLAND
STANDARD RELIGIOUS CEREMONY

In the Church of England you are married by a vicar. Banns are called in advance, and the vicar takes care of all documentation. No registrar's certificate is needed. At your own parish church you do not necessarily need a birth certificate if evidence of your age is on the parish register from your baptism.

BANNS

To ensure that forbidden marriages do not happen accidentally there are 'banns' or public announcements, followed by a delay of several weeks so news of the forthcoming marriage can spread. Anyone who knows a good reason why the couple should not marry could come forward. This is why banns are read out in church three Sundays in a row. Banns also deter bigamous marriages, which explains why banns are read in the home towns of both parties intending to marry. (Register offices check to ensure that bigamous marriages are not being entered into.)

CHURCH ETIQUETTE AND PUNCTUALITY

Ushers should arrive an hour in advance to show guests to their seats and hand out order-of-service sheets. Guests should arrive at least fifteen minutes in advance.

Guests should not arrive at church drunk, walk in laughing, nor walk in or out during the wedding ceremony. It is usual for the bride's friends and relatives to sit on the left-hand side of the church and for the groom's family and friends to sit on the right. Close family sit nearest the front.

The groom must be there, be on time, and be sober. The best man is responsible for this. The groom and best man wait by the altar at least half an hour in advance. The bridesmaids wait by the church door. (It is also possible to have the chief usher or best man by the church door. He goes inside to nod to the groom and vicar that the bride has arrived.) In many churches the vicar waits by the church door and precedes the bride in the procession.

The bride's mother arrives just before the bride and sits in the front pew on the left of the aisle. (After this nobody else enters.) Latecomers wait in the hallway or go upstairs to the gallery.

The bride's car may arrive five minutes early to allow time for photographs. The chauffeur opens the door for her father to alight in the road and her father goes round the back of the car to the kerb to help out the bride.

The bridegroom is waiting with the best man in the front right-hand pew. The vicar is at the altar rail.

A signal is given to the organist to start playing the music. On hearing the music the groom, best man and anyone else who was seated must stand upright.

PROCESSION ORDER

The bride with her father on her left proceeds up the left aisle, or the centre aisle if there is one. Tiny bridesmaids holding the train follow, then the chief bridesmaid. The bride's family are seated on the left of the aisle.

(NB. Orthodox Jewish weddings are slightly different. See below.)

The father escorts his daughter in the procession up the aisle, followed by the bridesmaids. The bride stops facing the altar, next to the groom who is now on her right. The chief bridesmaid stands behind the bride, and takes the bouqet and gloves, so that the bride is free to hold out her hand to receive the ring. The bride's father gives her away then steps back to sit with the bride's mother in the front pew.

The groom says his vows with his hand on the bride's. They release hands so that she can place hers above his when she makes her vow. In many churches the bride's veil is lifted immediately after the vows and exchange of rings when the vicar says to the groom, 'You may now kiss the bride'. Alternatively the veil can be lifted during the hymn, before the prayers or in the vestry.

The Russian and Greek Orthodox bind hands. So do the Anglo-Catholic who are high church, favouring statues, incense, and vestments.

TRADITIONAL AND MODERN CHURCH OF ENGLAND WEDDINGS

During the conventional church wedding you are required to disclaim knowledge of any impediment to marriage, and declare your consent. The marriage must take place between the hours of 8 am and 6 pm, with open doors, and two witnesses.

It is worthwhile for the couple to look at the choice of wording before meeting the minister, to avoid arguing with each other in front of him. Ministers, however, are usually diplomatic and may help you reach agreement.

The traditional wedding service is in the Book of

Common Prayer, available from bookshops, churches, cathedral bookshops, etc. The familiar service is in archaic language, 'Wilt thou have ... 'thy' wife, 'ye', etc.

The replies being 'I will', and 'I take thee' ...

The priest asks who 'giveth ...' and the father or friend steps forward to hand his daughter to the minister who sees that the groom's hand is placed on the bride's.

The ring is placed on the prayerbook, then the priest hands the ring to the groom. On placing the ring on the third finger of the bride's left hand the groom keeps his hand on the ring while he makes his statement and again archaic language is used, 'I thee wed', 'thee worship', and 'thee endow' ... etc.

More significant is the fact that the bride's response includes the word 'obey'. The couple kneel and a prayer is said while the rest of the congregation remain standing. Then the priest joins their hands and pronounces them married.

The bride and groom decide whether they are happy with the older language and find it more beautiful and meaningful. It is less important whether the congregation understand the vows.

The Alternative Service Book of 1980 contains the modern version, and inexpensive reprints of the marriage service alone can be obtained from bookshops such as Mowbrays near Oxford Circus, London, by mail order, and from SPCK, 112 Marylebone Road, London NW1.

The groom is asked 'will you' (take this woman) ... to be 'your wife?' and he replies, 'I will'. The bride follows the same procedure.

Other differences include using the word 'share' instead of 'endow'. The bride may omit the word 'obey'. The giving away is optional. The couple are pronounced married.

The signing may take place at this point or after an optional number of further hymns, psalms, prayers and blessings. Some couples also opt for an address.

RECESSION ORDER

For the recession, or return down the aisle, the bride is on the groom's left, so he has to move before leading her down the aisle, followed by the bridesmaids.

The bride returns down the right or centre aisle. Her husband is holding her right arm. Small bridesmaids hold the bride's train. The best man and chief bridesmaid follow behind. Finally come the bride's mother with the groom's father, then the bride's father with the groom's mother.

HYMNS, READINGS AND PRAYERS

For committed believers, hymns such as 'Jesus shall reign where'er the sun ...' can be very moving, adding significance to the occasion. If you have invited many non-Christians, they will be puzzled by a choice of hymns such as 'Stand Up, Stand Up For Jesus'. It is tactful to choose innocuous hymns such as 'All Things Bright and Beautiful' so that everyone can join in the singing. Old Testament readings and prayers will similarly be more familiar and acceptable to a mixed-faith congregation.

MUSIC

Some churches ban 'Here Comes the Bride' because it has become a cliché. Choose music which inspires reverence. If you know nothing about music, the vicar and the church organist will be happy to advise you. Remember you will have to choose some pieces to be played during the procession, recession and signing of the register, as well as the hymns.

CONFETTI AND BELLS

Well-wishers throw confetti over the bride and groom as they make their way to the car, especially at country churches with a walk from the church door to the church gate. Get permission from the church to throw confetti because some regard it as litter. If confetti is allowed, the chief bridesmaid and best man should agree who will be delegated to supply confetti to guests, so that the bride is not disappointed. If confetti is not allowed in the churchyard it is thrown as the couple emerge outside the church gate, using confetti made of a substance which can be eaten by birds.

Wedding bells are rung to announce that the bride is married. (Bell-ringers require payment.) In city centres crowds in the street will stop to see the bride being photographed on the church steps before she gets into the car.

PHOTOGRAPHS AND VIDEOS

Permission is required for photographs or video-recordings in churches and religious establishments. The minister may feel that the video camera will distract or detract from the religious atmosphere. He may permit photographs in church before and after the ceremony but not during the service.

Photographs before the service could include the bride getting out of the car, on the arm of whoever is giving her away, or with her bridesmaids who are waiting for her at the church door.

★ *GROUP PHOTOGRAPHS*   The majority of photographs will include the bride. She will be photographed on her own, with the groom, and with all the wedding group and various members of the wedding party such as her mother, her parents, the chief bridesmaid, or the matron-of-honour.

★ **WHOM TO PHOTOGRAPH**

The groom may wish to be photographed with the ushers. Other VIPs or guests of honour can have individual portraits and photographs with bride and groom or both. For example, the bride's mother, the bride's parents, the groom's parents, and both sets of parents. Don't forget VIPs outside the family – the friend who loaned the car photographed with the car, the person who made the cake photographed with the cake, and granny or nanny.

Photograph the speechmakers, the cake cutting, throwing the bouquet, raising glasses for toasts, and waving from the car with Just Married signs.

★ **PHOTOGRAPHS WITH CHILDREN**

Pretty photographs can be taken of junior bridesmaids and pages with the bride and groom, on their own, and with their parents. Don't let children jump into every photograph. Have bride and groom photographed separately before or after the wedding reception, and take photographs in different parts of the garden. While children pose with the bride, photograph the groom alone.

WRITING FOR INFORMATION

When writing to the Dean or Provost of a cathedral address him as The Very Revd. For more information check The Book of Common Prayer or contact the Church of England Enquiry Centre, Church House, Great Smith Street, Westminster, London SW1P 3NZ, tel. 01–222 9011.

CHURCH OF SCOTLAND, WEDDINGS IN SCOTLAND, AND SCOTTISH WEDDING RECEPTIONS

Four weeks in advance of the wedding (six weeks if you were previously married), take the money for the fees and your documents (birth certificates and any divorce decree or death certificate of former spouse) and deliver your marriage notices to the registrar. You must go to the Office of the Registrar fifteen days prior to the marriage (not more than three months prior). Return to collect the Marriage Schedule in the week before the wedding. (It cannot be given to you more than seven days earlier). It must be handed to the minister before the marriage service starts. The minister cannot proceed without the Marriage Schedule because it is a criminal offence to do so. (You could deliver it the day before in case you forget it on the day.)

The minister's fee is not always set; it is usually up to you. You may make a voluntary contribution to the church heating or lighting, or there may be a set fee. The organist and church officer usually receive a set fee.

The bridesmaid might journey to church with the bride or be taken there by the best man (after he has delivered the groom).

The Church of Scotland, the established or national

Church, is Presbyterian. Unlike the Church of England it is independent from the state. (Other Presbyterian Churches include the United Free Church.) You can be married by a man or woman minister, in a church or other building such as a home or hotel, at any time – late afternoon such as 4 pm or 5 pm being popular.

The groom may wait at the church door or by the communion table (there is no altar), at the minister's discretion. Ministers are described as The Reverend, not as Reverend which is an Americanism.

For more details about church weddings contact the Church of Scotland, 121 George Street, Edinburgh EH2 4YN, tel. 031–226 3405; or the Scottish Episcopal Church, tel. 031–225 6357.

You can marry in Scotland according to other faiths (e.g. Bahai) and in a register office. Scotland is considered romantic, especially the nearest point to the border, Gretna Green, formerly the destination of eloping couples. About one thousand five hundred marriages still take place every year at Gretna Green, although it is so small that the post is routed via Carlisle, just across the border in England. There is a long waiting list, so write to Gretna Green Register Office well in advance for details.

Scottish couples often choose to wear formal Scottish clothes even in daytime. A Scottish groom and other Scotsmen wear dress tartan kilts, an English best man or groom wears a morning coat, and Scottish bridesmaids wear plaid sashes. Girls in kilts wear black patent leather shoes with silver buckles. As the car leaves church, traditionally the couple throw coins and sweets to the local village children. Do not throw coins, sweets, bridal bouquets or anything else near a roadway where children will scramble, push and run near traffic.

A Scottish piper in a kilt can be at the reception

hotel playing outside the front door, in a courtyard, or on a balcony to welcome guests on arrival. Photographs should include the piper. During the reception the same piper can play reels. Scottish food such as haggis is served and malt whisky is popular.

A Scottish bagpipers' agency in London can supply a piper to play bagpipes in church during the signing of register and procession (in England get the vicar's permission).

The receiving line starts with the bride's parents, then the groom's parents, then the bridal couple, then the bridesmaid and finally the best man (ladies first all along the line).

Toasts and cake cutting precede the meal. Guests go to the tables first and bride and groom arrive last.

At the reception the minister sits on the bride's left, between the bride and the bride's mother. The bride's father is left of the bride's mother. Next comes the groom's mother, with the groom's father on the bride's far left. The bridegroom has a bridesmaid on his right with a best man at the end of the table.

The meal is followed by telegram reading, then another toast to the bridal couple, the groom's reply ending with toast to the bridesmaids, the best man's reply, and then maybe toasts to the couple's parents and/or speeches by them.

Some Scottish towns are dry (ban alcohol). In any case you should offer non-alcoholic drinks at the same time as alcoholic drinks so that for toasts and other occasions guests have a choice.

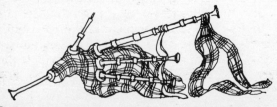

WELSH WEDDINGS

The ceremony will take place in Welsh if the bride and groom speak Welsh. The Church of Wales, and Welsh Congregational Churches in Wales or London can supply ceremony details which are similar to the English equivalents.

At the reception there are numerous speeches and then the floor is open to guests to make speeches, 'Would anyone else like to say a few words?' Dancing may include Welsh folk dancing, reels such as the Llanover Reel, harpists, choirs singing songs such as The Ashgrove, and bards reciting poems composed in the Welsh language mentioning the bride and groom.

METHODIST WEDDINGS

In the Free Churches you address the minister as 'Mr.' When speaking about him you refer to him in the third person as The Reverend. Address an envelope to him as The Reverend, but begin the letter with Dear Mr Smith, or whatever his name is. However, the minister is unlikely to be fussy about whether you get it right.

Brides wear white as is the custom. Bridesmaids may stand or sit, depending on their age. You can decide this at the rehearsal. No hats are necessary.

The administrator of my local United Reformed Methodist church explains that although traditionally the bride did not remove her veil until the end of the service, nowadays they ask the bride to remove her veil at the beginning. So check with your local church.

Historically, the foundation of the Methodists was linked to the temperance movement and no alcohol is allowed on the premises – a law which the minister cannot waive. Since most people like to serve alcohol at wedding receptions it is not common to hold receptions on Methodist premises.

QUAKER WEDDINGS

Sunday is not considered a particularly holy day though meetings are often held on Sunday for convenience. 'Friends' marriages are exempt from certain provisions of the Marriage Act (1949) such as registering the premises for marriage and you can marry in the bride's home if no Quaker Meeting House or regular meeting place is nearby. Quaker meetings are essentially democratic, with long periods of silent reflection broken when someone feels inspired to speak, read, or after due consideration to respond to another's thoughts or offer support. For example, on the occasion of a wedding an Elder might rise to reflect upon the blessings of marriage or ask for a blessing upon the couple. To create the right atmosphere they arrange for sufficient numbers of regular attenders to be present at a wedding so that guests unfamiliar with the ambience do not outnumber the others.

The bridal couple usually arrive in their own car since a Rolls-Royce is considered ostentatious. The bride wears no veil and need not dress in white. Best man and bridesmaids are not necessary. Morning coats are not usually worn by the men, just grey or dark suits and carnations. There is no procession or music. The bride's mother may have decorated the room with vases of flowers, possibly employing the help of a professional florist.

The bride and groom sit facing the meeting. The best man and bridesmaids, if any, sit beside them and the immediate family sit close to them. After a period of quiet, when a sense of harmony prevails, the couple hold hands. Both stand and recite promises. He speaks first. They promise to be 'loving and faithful'. There is a slight choice of wording – 'with God's help' or 'with divine assistance'. The form they both use is decided in advance in consultation with the Elders. A wedding ring is not necessary, but is often placed on the finger immediately after making the promises.

There is then a time of silent communion during which those attending may occasionally be inspired to express their thoughts and prayers. Meetings do not end after somebody has spoken but following a period of about half an hour's silence when an atmosphere of calm prevails. The meeting ends with two of the Elders of the Meeting shaking hands.

If the reception is held in an adjoining room all the worshippers join the bride and groom to share food the bride's family has provided. No alcohol is served. If the reception is held elsewhere only those specifically invited attend.

ROMAN CATHOLIC WEDDINGS

The Catholic Church requires a minimum of six months' notice to prepare the couple and prepare documents. The couple can be married by a bishop, priest, or deacon.

No head covering is required for bride or guests. Latin is no longer obligatory and mostly is not used, except in the mass where Latin is optional.

★ *PRELIMINARY QUESTIONS*   Three preliminary questions are asked including one about whether you are ready to bring up children according to the law of Christ and his Church (the response being, 'I am').

★ *MARRIAGE IMPEDIMENT DISCLAIMER*   You may say the words after the priest or read that you do not know of any impediment.

★ **DECLARATION**
OF CONSENT

The bride and groom declare consent ('I will').

★ **VOWS BEFORE**
WITNESSES

The couple join right hands (father placing bride's hand on groom's). The priest says the formulae which are repeated by the groom or bride, or vows may be read from the book.

The traditional 'For better for worse' formula is the same as that laid down for Church of England. The groom calls on the congregation to witness, and says the few words ending, 'till death do us part'. The couple separate their hands and rejoin them, and the bride says the words ending, 'till death do us part'.

★ **GIVING OF**
RINGS

The priest blesses the ring before it is placed on the bride's finger, or two rings are blessed before being exchanged. Traditionally the groom placed the wedding ring on the bride's thumb, saying, 'in the name of the father,' on the second finger saying, '. . . in the name of the son,' on the middle finger saying, 'and of the holy ghost,' finally on the third finger saying, 'Amen'. If two rings were used the bride then placed his ring on his fingers, following the same practice of placing it on one finger after the other, saying the same words. The groom may do this or place the ring directly on the bride's third finger, saying the above words.

After the solemnization of the marriage, i.e. the vows, there may be a nuptial mass during which either or both of the couple receive holy communion, consecrated wine and bread given only to baptized Catholics. A blessing is said over the newlyweds and they are sprinkled with holy water.

After the ceremony the bride and groom go to a table at one side to sign the register so they are still in view (or in the sacristy), and then stand so that the bride is on the groom's left for the recession.

You can read the exact wording in *The Rite of Marriage for use of congregations in The Diocese of England and Wales* which you can obtain by mail order from Mowbray's Bookshop in London, or from your local Catholic church. *The Rite of the Sacrament of Marriage* is published by the Catholic Truth Society.

If your family books are old, see the Roman Catholic mass revised in the 1960s (before that mass was in Latin). Check if there are later changes. The Code of Canon Law lists which marriages are forbidden, not necessarily the same as those disallowed by British or European law. Currently first cousin marriages are not allowed but you should check the latest rulings.

The priest may be invited to the wedding reception in which case he will say grace before the meal. A priest named John Brown would be addressed as Father Brown or Father John or simply Father. When you know him very well you might just call him John.

EUROPEAN CATHOLIC WEDDINGS

In Catholic countries such as Spain and Italy the

engagement ring is worn on the right hand during the engagement, and moved to the left hand on marriage. The same applies to Catholics in some non-Catholic countries such as Holland.

In France and most European countries the marriage contract is signed at the town hall before the church wedding.

In France and Italy divorcees and pregnant brides wear cream or pastel colour dresses. The groom enters church accompanied by his mother.

In Spain one parent of the bride accompanies one parent of the groom in the procession.

EASTERN OR GREEK ORTHODOX

Eastern Orthodox is a term used by the Greek Orthodox, and Ukranians (from Russia), also Syrian, and Coptic (from Egypt), who have varying practices. You will find current addresses of the Serbian (Yugo-slavian), Russian Orthodox and other churches in the London yellow pages under Place of Worship and Religious Organizations.

★ *GREEK ORTHODOX WEDDINGS*

Remember that the head of their Church is not the Pope but the Patriarch. The Greek bride, her father, and maid-of-honour may travel to church in the same car, the best man giving the bride her bouquet at the door. The bride usually wears white although this is not compulsory. The priest places crowns on the heads of bride and groom, and the ceremony is called crowning. The 'Father' – not the bride's father but a holy man, might marry them in a Greek Orthodox cathedral. Guests need not cover their heads.

At Greek Orthodox weddings there are many best men and best women or bridesmaids according to the couple's status. Attendants pay for the bride's dress and lead the first dance.

At the reception, it is a Greek/Cypriot custom to pin money on the bride.

★ *GREEK-CYPRIOT WEDDINGS*

On a Greek island wedding the whole village would be invited, so a London wedding with 500 guests is not uncommon. There are no bridesmaids but instead female representatives from different families called first lady, second lady, and so on, and each family decides who represents them. The wedding invitation goes to the head of the household and he decides who should attend.

★ *UKRANIAN*
  WEDDINGS

You could have three bridesmaids and three best men. The singing is in Ukranian. The couple wear a green wreath of myrtle on their heads. The couple's hands are tied together. The Guard of Honour could wear Cossack green and red.

At the reception the bride's mother greets the married couple with bread and salt. Your menu might include Chicken Kiev, honouring the Ukranian capital city in Russia. (For those who don't eat garlic offer an alternative dish.)

JEWISH WEDDINGS

The orthodox Jewish bride and her mother and mother-in-law arrive at the synagogue in the same car because the two women accompany her up the aisle. A Liberal or Reform synagogue's bride who advances up the aisle with her father arrives at the synagogue with him.

★ *THE JEWISH*
  MARRIAGE
  SERVICE

At orthodox Jewish weddings men and women sit separately. Head covering is required in the synagogue. The groom might wear a white satin cap. Usually a small paper skull cap will be provided for men who don't have velvet or silk skullcaps. Ladies wear hats. The bride is led in by both her mother and mother-in-law in the orthodox synagogue, by her father in the reform synagogue. The groom lifts her veil momentarily to check he is getting the right girl!

The prayer book has Hebrew on one side, English opposite, with instructions about when to stand. If you cannot follow, simply stand and sit when everybody else does. The ceremony takes place under a canopy representing the new home. The couple recite in Hebrew. The ring is placed on the bride's pointing finger of her right hand so everyone can see it. Later she transfers it to her left hand.

The groom breaks a glass under his foot. Everybody claps and shouts 'Mazel tov!' (good luck). Orthodox synagogues do not allow videos; some reform synagogues do.

The couple and the witnesses sign the register and are given a marriage certificate in Hebrew.

After the ceremony the bride and groom are left alone together in a synagogue room, no longer for consummating the marriage, just for a quick cuddle in private. Most couples do not wait but rush to the reception. One couple waited expectantly to be summoned, eventually locating the adjoining hall where the reception was proceeding merrily without them!

★ **WEDDING RECEPTIONS**

At the reception the rabbi says grace in Hebrew before and after the meal. Extended grace and songs with jolly choruses follow the meal. At ultra-orthodox wedding receptions men dance around the room in a big circle between courses, holding handkerchiefs so that one person does not touch another. Rousing music is played and the bride and groom are carried aloft on chairs.

At a large seated Jewish wedding a loyal toast is made to HM The Queen. This is because such toasts were common on formal occasions in past times. It also demonstrates that despite playing the national anthem of another country (Israel) later, the hosts and guests are loyal British subjects.

★ **KOSHER FOOD**

Provide Kosher food for guests. Meat and milk are not served at the same meal. Coffee is served black, or with a non-milk product, until several hours after meat. Following fish dinners you can have ice cream or cream desserts and coffee with cream.

AMERICAN WEDDINGS AND RECEPTIONS

Many states will not grant permission for marriage until supplied with documentation showing that both parties have had a medical test proving their blood is free of VD or AIDS symptoms, to protect children of the marriage.

Weddings feature small bridesmaids strewing rose petals in front of the bride and little children as ring-bearers with the rings on cushions. Ushers or grooms-men, and bridesmaids are paired off in the recession. Home weddings are permitted. Jewish couples can marry on the Sabbath (Saturday) in winter after dusk.

MUSLIM WEDDINGS

The bride will be dressed with many jewels and an elaborate heavy dress which may be any colour, perhaps a white saree and a garland. The bride can have a gold wedding ring. (Among some communities the groom's must be silver, not gold.)

The couple are seated in different rooms in the mosque, but symbolically sitting back to back. Two priests conduct the ceremony, beginning with a sermon on marriage and then the vows. Lady guests should cover their head, e.g. with a scarf, and their legs. Face and hands may be visible. Non-Muslims may enter the mosque.

When a wedding takes place in a mosque there will

be an hour or two spent at a reception there and then the ladies go to one house, the men to another.

Afterwards, sweets are given. Muslim guests eat Halal meat or vegetarian food, no pork. Rice and curry are popular. Orthodox Muslims do not drink alcohol so hosts should ensure a plentiful supply of non-alcoholic drinks, Coke, juices, etc. The groom's family gives presents to the bride's mother and the bride's family gives presents to the groom's mother. The gifts you give the wedding pair are the same as for any bridal couple, something for the home such as a clock or bedlinen.

Coins are thrown at the departing couple – make sure that coins do not damage the departure car.

HINDU WEDDINGS

A wedding car takes the groom with his sisters. The bride might wear red or pink, not usually white which is the colour of mourning and would be worn by a widow. The bride covers her head but guests need not. The engagement ceremony may take place on the first of the seven days of ceremonies, or the rings may have been exchanged earlier. Brothers and sisters have roles in the ceremonies. The couple walk around a fire in a basket seven times. Garlands are exchanged.

The reception is on the last day. Gifts of money end with the number one, e.g. £21 or £31. Customs of people from South India differ from those originating in North India. Not all Hindus are vegetarian but many are, so vegetarian food will be required at the reception held in the bride's mother's house or hotel.

SIKH WEDDINGS

Lady guests should cover their heads. Sikh women

wear saris with the ends over their heads or a Punjabi outfit with a knee-length dress, trousers and a long scarf to go over the head. Men may use a handkerchief or a hat. The orthodox Sikh observes five rules, wearing long hair, boxer shorts, a bangle, a comb in his hair and a dagger. Sikh men wear turbans over their long hair. A clean-shaven boy will grow a beard before the wedding and wear a turban.

A Sikh is married by a Garanthi or priest at a Sikh temple. The groom and male congregation gather in a forecourt or indoors in bad weather at 9 am or 10 am. The priest says a prayer of blessing. Equivalent members of each family meet and exchange garlands of tinsel, starting with the boy's father and girl's father (or uncle). Her brother meets his brother or cousin, and so on.

Guests are welcomed into the hall where they receive tea and vegetarian samosas (no meat is allowed in the temple), and sweets. Then everybody removes their shoes, and covers their head to move into the holy area, bowing their head on entering and putting money into a box for the temple, advancing to kneel and bow towards the book.

The groom sits on a blanket facing the holy book. The groom's father-in-law presents nuts and sweets to the groom and a gold bangle.

The bride wears a red or pink sari edged with gold thread embroidery, and has gold jewellery in her nose and on her forehead. Others remain seated while close female relatives lead in the bride who kneels and bows her head to the holy book and sits on the floor by the groom. The bride is expected to cry because she is leaving her parents' home forever to live in her mother-in-law's house. A familiar sister-in-law from her household (her brother's wife) or a married sister sits alongside to help and comfort her. The marriage promises are sung, accompanied by the music of small drums beaten with the hands. The priest sings hymns and musicians play a little drum and a kind of harmonium.

The bride's father gives the groom a long scarf symbolizing giving away the bride. Then the bride and groom rise and walk clockwise around the holy book four times, the groom leading the bride by the scarf which is draped over his shoulder. After standing for prayer, guests give sweets and money to the bride, about £5, in addition to wedding presents given previously. The money goes to the bride's mother-in-law. Elderly people put a hand on the head of boy and girl to bless them after giving them money. Guests bow their heads to the holy book.

The couple sign the Sikh wedding book while guests depart for the reception held in a hall. The food for as many as 400 people may be made by family and friends and consists of chapatis, vegetable samosas, puris, curries and so on. Alcohol is served. The bride returns to her parents' home, from which the groom and his immediate family collect her.

BAHAI WEDDINGS

There are no arranged marriages. The bride and groom must get the consent of all living parents, because weddings are considered to be uniting families. Parents who do not consent may be persuaded to change their minds. But having given consent they cannot withdraw it afterwards.

There are no ritual requirements, except reciting, 'Verily we are content with the will of God'. The bride and groom can read poetry or play music. There are no rules about dress – except that clothing tends to be fairly modest. The bride can wear white, which is popular, but a red sari would be equally acceptable or any other suitable attire, and a best man and brides-maids can take part. There are no rules about food except that no alcohol is drunk.

BUDDHIST WEDDINGS (SRI LANKA)

The bride wears a white dress or sari, worn draped over the opposite shoulder to the Indian sari, with frills at waist level, and seven necklace chains.

ORIENTAL WEDDINGS

Chinese wedding cars are decorated with a doll dressed in bridal costume on the bonnet and balloons.

The Japanese wrap money, including tips, in fancy envelopes. Shoes should be removed on entering the home.

DOUBLE WEDDINGS

When you have a double wedding, both couples should

be treated equally. But walking up the aisle in the procession, somebody has to go first, so that is the eldest groom, and in most cases he is with the eldest bride as well.

At the reception held by the bride's parents, if the two brides are sisters, generally the eldest bride takes precedence.

THE RECEPTION

After the ceremony itself, the reception is one of the most memorable parts of the wedding day. Do make sure you know what to expect, and when.

TRANSPORT TO THE RECEPTION

The chauffeur opens the car door or doors in advance. The bride and groom depart first. Usually the car is parked in the direction of the traffic. The groom gets in first from the kerbside (which is safer) and moves across. The bride is helped in by bridesmaids and sits on the left of the groom. The photographer snaps them, with the bride nearest the camera.

Occasionally a bride with a long train gets in first and moves to the far side of the car so there is room for the train to follow her. The groom then gets in. The best man shuts the car door. In a car park the photographer and guests can see the bride from the driver's side.

The best man stays until last to organize the cars unless he is needed to announce guests arriving at the wedding reception. If so, the chief usher can direct cars.

On arriving at the reception, if there is no hotel porter, the chauffeur opens the door for the groom who alights first and goes round the car to help out his bride. Hotels which hold many wedding receptions lay out a red carpet under an awning up to the hotel door. Bridesmaids who arrive at the reception just behind the bride stand ahead of the bride ready to help her through the hall door.

A wedding reception held at a private house may be harder for guests to find than a hall on a main road. Send maps with directions. Ushers should direct the cars. You may need one usher at the end of the road, or a recognizable sign such as a wedding bell and arrow indicating where they turn off the main road into a side road. An usher should be at the house driveway assuring drivers that they have found the right place. If it rains, an usher with an umbrella opens car doors and helps ladies and passengers to alight.

CAR PARKING AT HOME

It is a courtesy to inform the neighbours that many cars will park on the road near your house on the wedding day. Apologize for any inconvenience, and say that if driveways are obstructed they should inform you at once so you can remedy the problem. Invite neighbours to the reception. When a family who lived in a cul-de-sac did so, thoughtful neighbours kept their cars in garages, allowing visitors to park on forecourts.

THE RECEIVING LINE

At a large gathering a receiving line is arranged so that arriving guests are all welcomed by their hosts and speak to the bride. Where a hotel has several weddings on the same day, a toastmaster may be needed to organize each group. Hosts should arrive first, before the guests. The bridal couple must avoid being unduly delayed by the photographer.

The traditional arrangement has the hosts first, bride's mother and father, groom's mother and father, finally the bride and groom. This works well at the bride's mothers home when most of the guests know her. Here it is best to have the bride and groom last, particularly if they are meeting strangers who can be greeted by name by the parents.

You can speed up the receiving line by having just the bride and groom at the door. Have the bride first if she is an older bride welcoming guests to a reception in her new home. Bride and groom are first, then the bride's mother and father (or stepfather if he is contributing to the wedding and acting as host), then the groom's mother and father.

The best man and bridesmaids do not usually stand in the receiving line, except perhaps if they are the brothers and sisters of the bride or groom.

At formal weddings the toastmaster announces the guests. Guests should keep in family groups as they approach the receiving line. This helps the bride later with introductions. At my wedding I introduced a cousin from Manchester to another Manchester cousin. They looked so surprised. They were brothers!

Hosts say, 'Lovely to see you, Auntie Ann ... I'm so glad you could be with us.' Guests say, 'What a beautiful wedding.' To the bride they could say: 'You look really lovely. Congratulations and lots of happiness.' The bride replies, 'Thank you so much.'

Guests should not hold up the receiving line with extended chat. If they do the hosts can usher them on tactfully, 'Do go and have a drink, Auntie Ann. I'll have a long chat with you later.'

RECEPTION DRINKS

Hosts do not want guests to wait for food and drink. At

a large function there may be a long delay before guests reach the end of the receiving line. Usually drinks and nibbles are distributed by the caterers before people sit down to a meal because nobody can start until the hosts have finished greeting guests.

The layout of the premises influences where and when guests receive drinks. At a home reception, where the receiving line is in the back garden, hosts can instruct caterers to offer drinks to guests on arrival at the house. Guests approach the receiving line with drinks in their left hand in order to shake hands with their right.

SEATING PLANS

In addition to place-cards on tables, for a large hall you need a seating plan. This can be mounted on a blackboard at the dining area entrance, firmly attached so that the throng of people trying to see do not knock it over. The writing should be large enough for people to read without glasses. It can be decorated with hearts or wedding bells and kept as a souvenir.

The closest family who are anxious to be near the bride sit at tables in front of the top table or nearest to it. Place distant cousins further away at tables in the nearest row on the far left and right. Friends and colleagues who know only one side of the family, and children, can sit at the back of the hall.

Don't sit down and start eating straight away. If the ceremony was a church one, the minister is invited to say grace before meals. The toastmaster announces, 'Pray silence for ... who will now say grace.'

CAKE CUTTING

After a buffet the cake is cut and then speeches are made. At a seated dinner often no one has room for cake immediately after the dessert. Speeches are held at the end of the meal and the cake can be cut later in the evening.

The caterer packages up leftover cake which the bride's mother can take home and cut into small pieces for distribution. Sometimes the caterer cuts the cake, placing pieces in small boxes decorated with silver bells, and the names of the bride and groom on a card, to be posted to those unable to attend the wedding who sent telegrams or gifts.

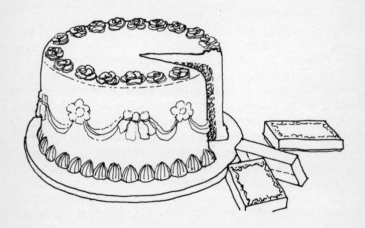

Later if guests stay for dancing, coffee and tea are served with cakes or small Danish pastries, followed by petit fours.

SMOKING

Even if hosts provide cigarettes in glamorous coloured wrappers with gold tips, and cigars, to ensure that guests need not supply anything, do not smoke until everybody has finished eating. Smoke interferes with the aroma of food.

The signal that you can smoke is given by the toastmaster who says, 'Ladies and Gentlemen, you may now smoke.' Ask whether anyone prefers you not to smoke, and offer to change places so that a non-smoker is not stuck between smokers. Do not smoke beside children, or guests who have given up smoking, or suffer from colds and hay fever.

TOASTS AND SPEECHES

To get silence for speeches the toastmaster, or whoever is giving the first speech, can bang a mallet on the table.

ORDER OF SPEECHES

The first speech is the toast to the happy couple by the bride's father. If he is deceased, unable, or unwilling to speak, an uncle or friend of the family can give this speech. Or the bride's mother could speak if her husband is unwell or hard of hearing. The groom replies and thanks his in-laws as hosts, with a toast to them and to the bridesmaids. The best man replies on behalf of the bridesmaids.

★ *FIRST SPEECH*   Work out who must be praised and thanked. For example, the first speechmaker, either the father of the bride or a family friend, gives a speech honouring the VIPs of the day, the father praising the groom, the family friend praising the groom first but often both of the young couple, finishing with a toast to the bride and groom.

★ **SECOND SPEECH**   One speech flows into the next. Naturally, the groom rises to his feet to thank the previous speaker. But the main purpose of the groom's speech (and/or bride's speech) is to thank those who have contributed to the day, the bridesmaids, or if there are no bridesmaids, the hosts. So the groom ends with a toast to the bridesmaids, or to the hosts, traditionally the bride's parents. Nowadays the groom's parents have often made a contribution to the wedding and they will be mentioned in the groom's speech and toasts too, especially if they are present.

★ **THIRD SPEECH**   If a friend of the family spoke first, an extra speech may be made by the host (bride's father) thanking the attendants, the best man and bridesmaids, ending with a toast, perhaps to the groom's parents.

The usual third speech is the best man replying on behalf of the bridesmaids, ending with reading telegrams.

If the circumstances of the wedding are different obviously you change the speeches accordingly. The important thing is to praise the bride and groom, thank the host, and attendants. Most guests also want to hear the groom say something.

★ **WHAT TO INCLUDE**

Follow on from the previous speaker, if any. You can assume that your audience will agree if you declare that the bride is pretty and that the host is a wonderful person. Say something original and informative about their good qualities. Humorous quotations to get attention at the start of the speech can be found in reference books. A popular subject for authoritative speakers such as ministers of religion is rules for a happy marriage — preferably funny rules! Finish with the toast.

★ **TELEGRAMS**

Telegrams are read by the toastmaster, if there is one, or by the best man. Read them in order of importance, close relatives such as the beloved brother living abroad before mere acquaintances. If several repeat the same greeting read or paraphrase it once and mention well-wishers' names explaining who's who. For example, 'There are good wishes from Arthur's Uncle Alex in Australia, and all the girls at Woolworth's where Anna works on Saturdays.' Keep the telegrams so that the senders can be thanked later. If there are few telegrams conceal this by reading humorous spoof messages, such as, 'Hilda says, Good luck, Harry. I trust I'll still see you Thursdays.'

★ *OTHER ANNOUNCEMENTS* The bride is the VIP. Guests should not announce engagements or otherwise divert attention from her without her prior approval. She may wish to announce her sister's engagement or a favourite aunt's birthday and present a bouquet.

DANCING

The bride and groom start the first dance. For the second dance bride and groom could separate. The bride might dance with her father while the groom dances with her mother. For the third dance the bride and groom could partner the groom's parents.

Another system is for the toastmaster to call the bride and groom to dance first. After they have circled the dance floor once, call the bride's parents to join them, then the groom's parents, next the ushers and bridesmaids, finally all the guests. The last dance is the bride and groom dancing the last waltz together, or end with Auld Lang Syne.

CATERING AT HOME

A home wedding can be catered with waitresses, waiters and a barman, leaving hosts free to mingle. Otherwise, for an even less formal event, bridesmaids pass around buffet food and wedding cake; ushers serve drinks; and attendants who notice a shortage of clean glasses point this out, washing a few or take clean ones from cupboards.

One couple who opted for this informal style even asked their guests to bring along items of food, and served up a summer picnic in their garden.

WEDDING GIFT DISPLAY

When a wedding is held at the bride's mother's or the new home the gifts can be displayed on a large table. If you are short of space put out one place setting from each tea set or dinner service. The card can read, From (donor's name) A Tea Set. This prevents a dinner service dominating the table. Gifts which co-ordinate well can be placed together. Similar gifts, and those of disparate cost or style, are best widely separated. Sealed envelopes are marked, From (name) A Cheque, or House Deposit.

★ *THANK YOU NOTES*

Acknowledge cheques by thanking the donor for 'your generous gift/cheque' without specifying the amount.

★ *PRESENTATION OF GIFTS*

Gifts to the attendants may be presented before the wedding if items they can wear at the wedding – jewellery for instance – are chosen. Alternatively, gifts can be presented during the wedding, or afterwards.

The bride's mother is often given a bouquet at the wedding reception. It is nice to be presented with a bouquet in public. However, a bride's mother who has a garden and gets the table displays might prefer a gift she can wear or display proudly at home as 'a present from my daughter and son-in-law'.

★ *EXCHANGING DUPLICATE GIFTS*

Suppliers of unwanted gifts can be found by the bride's mother asking the donor where the gift was bought, tactfully claiming other relatives admired it and want something similar. Considerate guests say where they obtained gifts, 'In case you want to exchange something'. The bride obviously assures them she doesn't, but notes down the shop names to replace breakages. (With a wedding list at a particular store, duplication and the supply of unwanted gifts should not occur).

★ *DELIVERY OF GIFTS*

Guests should send the gift before the wedding date. Taking gifts to the reception is an inconvenience. It is too late to put gifts on the wedding gift display. It looks as though you wanted to save delivery costs or to be sure of attending the wedding before you handed over the present. Gifts can go astray at the hall and be stolen from car parks.

The bride throws her bouquet, often from the top of the stairs as she goes up to change to go away. Bridesmaids or unmarried girls run to catch it and whoever does so is supposed to be the next bride. Or the bride can throw her bouquet as she enters the car to depart on honeymoon. The bride can save a bouquet made of silk flowers, or give it to a hospital or sick relative.

GOING AWAY

Guests should, out of politeness, stay until the bride and groom have left the reception. The time between arriving at the reception and going away will obviously vary from family to family. It may also depend on the type of reception or pressure from hotel staff or caterers to wind-up the festivities. For a day-time reception the bride should perhaps slip away to change after about one and half hours, maybe longer for an evening event where a dinner and dancing are involved.

During the reception the attendants surreptitiously decorate the wedding departure car so that it is a pleasant surprise. Old boots or shoes are tied to the back of the car.

AFTER THE WEDDING

After the wedding day there are still a few things to remember!

MARRIAGE ANNOUNCEMENTS

Bridesmaids can be listed in which case those over sixteen are prefixed by the title Miss, those under sixteen just have their first and last names given. Ushers are not normally mentioned. Pageboys have their first names and last names given. The term Master is no longer current. Use the prefix Mr for boys over the age of sixteen. Regular churchgoers mention the vicar if he is a family friend.

The honeymoon location is given if it is exotic. Simply say the honeymoon will be spent abroad if you prefer privacy from friends holidaying nearby, or are touring with no fixed address.

THE HONEYMOON

Traditionally the honeymoon destination is kept a secret to ensure privacy and avoid practical jokes. Secrecy cannot prevent confetti being scattered throughout the luggage so that the bride's clothes drop giveaway signals everywhere. But the best man is honour-bound to reveal practical jokes to the groom reasonably quickly – after the five minutes of fun.

SECOND HONEYMOON AND STEPCHILDREN

On a romantic honeymoon do not take your mother, mother-in-law, or your children from previous marriages. However, if both partners have children who cannot easily be left for the duration of a holiday, and look forward to being a family, you could honeymoon with *both* sets of stepchildren.

THE NEW HOME

When the bride and groom return to their new home together the bride is carried over the threshold for good luck so that she does not stumble. A groom who plans to carry his bride across the threshold should have a camera handy and call a photographer.

Formerly, brides sent out New Address cards giving an At Home day. Nowadays, phones encourage flexibility. Invite family, then friends, bride's parents first, especially if they bought the house, but groom's parents living nearer might consider they have precedence. To avoid offending either it is sensible to invite both families together. Everybody tours and admires the new house. If you are entertaining wedding guests, take care to display and use their gifts prominently.

Make sure you have seen the video before showing it to family and friends, and edit it. While a two-hour video may be fascinating to you it could be extremely boring for others. It could also have some embarrassing moments. One wedding video showed a guest at a European-style wedding removing money pinned to the bride's dress! A honeymoon video of an exotic destination was a disappointing blank except for flashing lights. Polite guests made a joke of the situation by thanking the hosts for showing a censored honeymoon film.

Take care when showing visitors your wedding photos – not all of them may have the patience or interest to sift through hundreds of pictures of you *however* stunning you look. They may equally all want to order prints of their favourite pictures, which can turn into an administrative chore of some magnitude.

Remember when you return to your new home and wedding gifts to write and thank all those guests who contributed to the dinner service or bought a wheelbarrow. The rules of etiquette don't stop once you're married!

WEDDING ANNIVERSARIES

Note your own and your in-laws' wedding anniversaries in your diary and send spouse and in-laws a card or gift. If you forget, Interflora send flowers the same day from a flower shop near the recipient's home (worldwide), reminding you to select a personal message to be handwritten on the printed card.

Newsagents and stationery shops stock invitation pads for silver, ruby, and golden weddings.

HAPPY ANNIVERSARY!

Here are your anniversaries:

FIRST ANNIVERSARY	— cotton
SECOND	— paper
THIRD	— leather
FOURTH	— fruit and flowers
FIFTH	— wooden
SIXTH	— sugar
SEVENTH	— woollen
TENTH	— tin
TWELFTH	— silk and linen
FIFTEENTH	— crystal
TWENTIETH	— china
TWENTY-FIFTH	— silver wedding
THIRTIETH	— pearl wedding
FORTIETH	— ruby wedding
FIFTIETH	— golden wedding
SIXTIETH	— diamond wedding – time to look back nostalgically at those lovely wedding photos

INDEX

THE FAMILY MATTERS SERIES

Anniversary Celebrations 0 7063 6636 0
Baby's First Year 0 7063 6778 2
Baby's Names and Star Signs 0 7063 6801 0
Baby's Names 0 7063 6542 9
Card Games 0 7063 6635 2
Card Games for One 0 7063 6747 2
Card and Conjuring Tricks 0 7063 6811 8
Charades and Party Games 0 7063 6637 9
Children's Party Games 0 7063 6611 5
Dreams and Their Meanings 0 7063 6802 9
Early Learning Games 0 7063 6771 5
Handwriting Secrets Revealed 0 7063 6841 X
How to be the Best Man 0 7063 6748 0
Microwave Tips and Timings 0 7063 6812 6
Modern Etiquette 0 7063 6641 7
Naming Baby 0 7063 5854 6
Palmistry 0 7063 6894 0
Successful Children's Parties 0 7063 6843 6
Travel Games 0 7063 6643 3
Wedding Planner 0 7063 6867 3
Wedding Speeches and Toasts 0 7063 6642 5